McGRAW-HILL READING

JUST THE THING

Authors

Elizabeth Sulzby
The University of Michigan

James Hoffman
University of Texas at Austin

Jerome Niles
Virginia Polytechnic Institute

Timothy Shanahan
University of Illinois at Chicago

William H. Teale
University of Texas at San Antonio

Literature Consultant

Sylvia Peña
University of Houston

Contributing Authors

Lillian K. Boyd
Detroit Public Schools

Kay M. Kincade
Central State University,
Edmond, Oklahoma

Jacqueline Kiraithe de Córdova
California State University
at Fullerton

Leon Lessinger, CEO
Health Champions, Inc.
Beverly Hills, California

Charles Mangrum II
University of Miami,
Coral Gables, Florida

George Mason
University of Georgia

Kathleen Naylor
Educational Consultant
Brea, California

Karen S. Urbschat
Wayne County Intermediate
School District, Michigan

Arnold Webb
Research For Better Schools
Philadelphia, Pennsylvania

Nancy G. Whisler
Richmond Unified School District,
California

McGraw-Hill School Division

New York   Oklahoma City   St. Louis   San Francisco   Dallas   Atlanta

The title of this book, "Just The Thing," is taken from the story "Just The Thing For Geraldine" by Ellen Conford.

Cover Illustration: Loretta Lustig

ISBN 0-07-042076-9

McGraw-Hill School Division
1200 Northwest 63rd Street
Oklahoma City, Oklahoma 73116-5712

2 3 4 5 6 7 8 9 0—8 9 7 6 5 4 3 2 1 0 9 8

Contents

Part One Close to Home

◇ Award-winning
book or
author

4

Part Two   Far Away

Part Three Learning

◇ Award-winning
book or
author

6

Part Four Growing

When You Read

I like to read.
Reading is fun.
I know some ways to help you read better.

Before You Read

Read the name of the story.
Look at the pictures.
Think about what you will read.

As You Read

- Stop after each page.
- Think about what you are reading.
- Think about what could come next.

Sometimes you see a word you do not know.
Try this.
1. Try to say the word.
2. Read the words before and after the word.
3. Look up the word in the Pictionary in the back of the book.
4. Ask for help.

After You Read
- Tell about the story.

Mitchell Is Moving

PART ONE

Close
to Home

I don't want you to move away.

Using Words About Homes

Look at the homes in the picture.
Who would you find in each home?
What other homes for people and
animals can you think of?
What can people and animals do at
home?
What can they do close to home?

Make a Story

Use words about homes and things
that are close to home to finish
the story.

One cold day, Pat stayed in the _____.
She found a _____ to play with.
When Pat's sister came home,
they _____.

As You Read

In this part of the book you will
read about things that are close to
home.
You will read about some people and
an animal and what they do at home.

Keep a Reader's Log.
You can write in the names of homes
and things that are close to home that
you know about.
Make notes in the log about what you
read.
If you find new words in the stories
you read, you can put them in the log.

What Will I Do at Home?

I have to stay at home today.
What will I do?
I am afraid that staying at home might
be dull.
Can you think of something fun that I
can do?

I could read, but what will I read
about?
I can think of hundreds of fun things
I could read about.
Maybe I will read.

14

I might paint, too.
There are hundreds of things I
could paint today.
Can you think of something that
I could paint?

I might play a game.
There are hundreds and hundreds of
things I might do at home!
Staying at home might not be so dull.
I can always think of something to do.

15

Strange Bumps

by Arnold Lobel

Owl was in bed.
"It is time to go to sleep," he said
with a yawn.

Then Owl saw two bumps under the
blanket at the end of his bed.
Owl was afraid.
"What can those strange bumps be?"
asked Owl.

Owl looked under the blanket.
He looked down into the bed.
It was dark.
Owl wanted to get some rest, but
he could not.

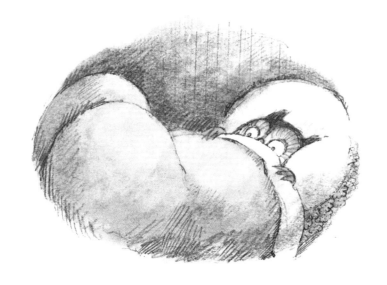

"Those strange bumps might get
big when I am sleeping," said Owl.
"That would not be nice."

Owl moved his feet up and down.
The bumps moved up and down.
"Look at those bumps move!" said Owl.

He moved his feet up and down again.
"Look at those bumps move again!"
cried Owl.

Owl pulled all of the blankets from
his bed.
The bumps were not there.
All Owl could see at the end of the bed
were his two feet.
Owl was not afraid now.

"But now I am cold," said Owl.
"I will put the blankets on the
bed again."

As soon as he did, he saw the same
two bumps.

"Those same bumps are back!" cried Owl.
"Bumps, bumps, bumps!
I will never get rest!"

Owl jumped up and down on top of
his bed.
"Where are you?" he cried.

With a bang the bed came falling down.
And with a bang Owl went falling
down on top of it.
Owl ran away from the bed.

He sat down in his chair and said,
"I will let those two strange bumps sit
on my bed.
Let the bumps grow as big as they wish.
I will sleep in my chair where I
am safe."

And that is what he did.

After You Read

Think

1. Why couldn't Owl go to sleep?

2. Did Owl get rid of the strange bumps?

3. What were the strange bumps in Owl's bed?

Share

What if you were Owl's friend?
What could you have said to help him?

Write

Owl was happy in his chair.
Write a sentence.
Tell something you do at home that makes you happy.

Read

You can read more stories about Owl in "Owl at Home," by Arnold Lobel.

First Pink Light

by Eloise Greenfield

Tyree put the last piece of a box on the
chair and looked at it.
Then he hid under the chair and
looked out.
He couldn't see his mother studying,
and she couldn't see him.

24

"Mama," he said, "you don't know where I am."

"Where are you?" his mother said.

"Don't be afraid.
I am in a place where I can hide,"
Tyree said.

"You are?" his mother said.
"Well, you have to come out.
It is time for you to go to bed."

"Don't forget, Daddy will be home!
I can't go to bed now," he said.

"Now you know I didn't forget that,
Tyree," she said.
"But it will be very late when your
daddy gets home."

"I know it," Tyree said, "but I want
to surprise him.
I have to stay in here and hide.
Then I will run to see him."

"You want to stay there all night long?" his mother asked.

"Yes, Mama, I want to stay here. I will not get tired," Tyree said.

"No, Tyree, you have to go to bed," his mother said.
"Your daddy will wake you up when he gets home."

"I don't want him to wake me up!" Tyree yelled.

His mother didn't know how he
felt.
His daddy had left to take care of
Grandpa.
He was away for a long time.
Now that Grandpa was better and
Daddy could come back home, Tyree
wanted to stay up to see him.
Tyree didn't want to go to sleep.
He didn't want his daddy to wake
him up.

"I can't go to bed!" he cried.
"I have to wait here for Daddy!"

His mother got up from studying.
"Now, Tyree," she said.
"If you sit here in the big chair, you
can stay up.
Then, when it is time for your daddy
to come home, you can leave the chair
and you can surprise him."

Tyree said, "I will not know when
it is time."

"Yes, you will," his mother said.
"I will show you.
Now look at the sky.
What do you see?"

"I just see dark," he said.

"Well, when it is time, you will
see something," his mother said.
"Because when the sun comes out,
a pink light comes out first.
So you can sit and look, and when
you see the first pink light, it will
be time to hide."

30

"Good," Tyree said.
"That is good."
Tyree jumped into the big chair.

Then his mother said, "Wouldn't you
like your blanket now?"

He got his blanket and sat down with
it in the chair.
It felt good.

He looked at the sky.
As soon as he saw the first pink
light, he would get in the place
where he would hide.
Then he would say, "Daddy," and his
daddy would hear him and find him.
Tyree was happy, thinking about how
he would jump into his daddy's arms
and how his daddy would carry him.
He sat in the chair and looked at
the sky for a long time.
His mother went on studying.

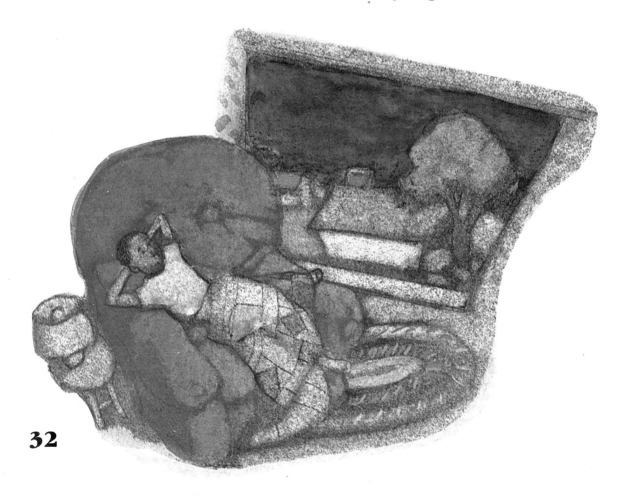

He looked and looked but the sky
stayed dark.
As it got late he got more and more
tired.
At last he went to sleep.
Tyree was sleeping when the sun
put its first pink light in the sky.

And he never hid under the chair to
surprise his daddy.
And he didn't hear or see his daddy
come in.
Tyree's daddy looked at Tyree
for a long, long time.

Tyree was still sleeping when he felt
a big, strong hand on his arm.
All the time he was reaching out
to his daddy, his daddy was
carrying him to bed.
All the time he was wishing that
his daddy would never have to leave
again, Tyree never woke up.

After You Read

Think

1. What did Tyree want to do?

2. What did the first pink light in the sky show?

3. Did Tyree stay up all night?

Share

Did Tyree's mother think that Tyree would stay up to see the first pink light?

Write

Write a sentence.
Tell about something that you would like to stay up late to see or do.

Read

If you liked this story, you might like to read ''Ira Sleeps Over,'' by Bernard Waber.

Eunice in the Evening

What is so nice in the dining room
Is—Everybody's There!
Daddy on the long settee—
A child in every chair—
Mama pouring cocoa in
The little cups of blue.
(And each of us has leave to take
A ginger cookie, too.)

Gwendolyn Brooks

Understanding
Order in a Story

Many things in stories happen in order.
Words like first, next, and last help you to know the order.

for **Too Many Books** and **Lizzie and Harold**

Thinking About Order

Read the story about Maria.
Look for the words that tell you the order of the things that happen.

Maria wanted to read a book.
First, she picked up the book she wanted to read.
Next, she sat down to read the book.
Last, she told Dad about the book.

As You Read

Ask yourself: In what order do things happen in the next two stories?

Use the words in blue to help you.

Too Many Books

by Caroline Feller Bauer

This story is about Maralou. Think about what she likes to do.

Maralou loved books, from the time she was a small baby.
She loved to learn.
When Maralou learned to read, she would read all of the time.
She always would read everywhere, at home and in town.

Each week, Maralou would go to the library to get books.
The next week, Maralou would go to bring the books back and get more.

The word **next** helps you know the order.

One day, Aunt Molly gave
Maralou a book.
What a surprise!
Aunt Molly was wonderful!
Now that Maralou owned a book, she
could study it and read it again
and again.

Maralou got
many books.
Think about
what will
happen next.

Maralou wanted more books.
She asked for books all the time.
She got many, many books as gifts
from Mom, Dad, and Aunt Molly.

As time went on, Maralou owned
a lot of books.

Mom, Dad, and Aunt Molly said
there wasn't room for all of the books.
The books did not fit in the house!

Maralou had too many books!
Mom couldn't get out of the house.
Dad couldn't get into the house.

But Maralou still loved books and
wanted more books to read.
Where could she make room for the
books?

Then Maralou had an idea.
Maybe more people loved to learn
from books!
So she started to give some books
away.

Look for the
words that help
you know the
order.

First, she gave a book to a small
boy who was going to school.
Next, she gave a book to a man on
the street.
Then, she left books everywhere.

Soon everyone in town was reading
all the time.
People started to trade books.

42

There were too many books to fit
in the town.

At last, a man called the people in
the library in a nearby town.

He wanted to see if the people in
that library would like to have
some books.

Last is a word
that helps you
know order.

They did, and soon all the towns
around were getting books.

Then they would call the people in
a nearby town to see if they
wanted books.

They always did.

Everyone was reading and learning
in all the towns around.

Think about how
the story will
end.

43

But Maralou didn't see all of this.
She sat by the library . . .
reading a book.

After You Read

Think

1. What did Maralou like to do best?

2. How did Maralou get so many books?

3. What did Maralou do for the people of the town?

Share

What are some books that you like to read?

Write

Write a list.
List the things you do to
take a book out of the library.
Use first, next, and last.

Read

If you liked this story, you might like
to read "Corduroy," by Don
Freeman.

Lizzie and Harold

by Elizabeth Winthrop

Lizzie wanted a best friend right away.
"Today I am going to find my best friend," Lizzie told Harold.

Harold lived next door.
Every day they walked to school together.

"Why do you want a best friend?" Harold asked.

"Because I need someone to tell secrets to and I want someone who likes me as much as I like her," Lizzie said.

"I will be your best friend,"
Harold said.

"You can't be," Lizzie said.
"You are a boy."

"So what?" said Harold.
But Lizzie did not answer.

The next day Lizzie wore a pink
flowered dress and black party shoes
to school.

"You look funny," Harold said.

"I look like Christina," Lizzie answered.
"She is going to be my new best friend."

"I like you best when you look like Lizzie," Harold said.

When Lizzie got to school, she ran up to Christina.

"I am wearing a dress and party shoes
just like you," said Lizzie.
"I want you to be my best friend."

"I don't want a best friend,"
Christina said.

"You don't?" said Lizzie.

"No," said Christina.
She walked away.

"How is your new friend?" Harold asked on the way home.

"Don't ask," said Lizzie. "Christina is not my best friend after all."

"That was quick," said Harold.

The next day, Lizzie put a sign on the door of her house.
The door bell rang.
Lizzie ran to open it.

There stood Harold.

"Here I am," he said.
"Your new best friend."

"You can't be my best friend," Lizzie
said.
"You are a boy."

Nobody else rang the door bell.
Lizzie took down the sign.

On the sign on the door:

Wanted
One Best
Friend.
Please ring
the
door bell.

"Does that mean that I am your best friend now?" Harold asked.

"No," said Lizzie.
"That means I give up.
I don't want a best friend after all."

The next day Harold was carrying a big blue bag to school.

"What is in your bag?" asked Lizzie.

"It is my trick-or-treat candy," said Harold.

"Why are you taking it to school?"
asked Lizzie.

"I am going to give it to the person
who promises to be my best friend,"
said Harold.
"Since you don't want to be my best
friend, I am going to find somebody
else."

"Harold, you can't find a best friend
that way," Lizzie said.

"Why not?" asked Harold.

"Because best friends just happen to you.
Besides, I thought you wanted to be my best friend," Lizzie cried.

But Harold wasn't listening.

All day long Lizzie thought about Harold.
When she met him after school, he did not have his blue bag of candy.

"I have a new best friend," Harold
said.
"He is a boy.
He ate all my candy and his name is
Douglas."

"Why do you look so sad?" Lizzie
asked.

"Because I like you better," said Harold.

"Well, I have a new best friend too,"
Lizzie said.
"He is a boy,
He likes me as much as I like him."

Harold looked even sadder.
"What is his name?" Harold asked.

"Harold," said Lizzie.

After You Read

Think

1. Why didn't Lizzie want Harold as a best friend at first?

2. What did Lizzie and Harold do to try to get best friends?

3. Who did Lizzie's best friend turn out to be?

Share

What makes a friend your best friend?

Write

Write an ending for the sentence.
You know someone is your best friend when ____.

Read

Read more about good friends in ''George and Martha, What Do You See?'' by James Marshall.

MAKING ALL THE
CONNECTIONS

Talk About It

Look at the picture.
Think about the stories in this
part of the book.
Think about the people and the
animal in the stories.
What did they do at home?
What did they do close to home?
What were the homes like?

Strange Bumps

First Pink Light

Too Many Books

Lizzie and Harold

Make a Plan of a Home

What kind of a home do you like?
Draw a picture of a home.
You can draw a picture of a home for
you, or a home for Owl, or for one of
the people in the stories.

1. Think about the kind of home
   you want to draw.
2. Draw the home.
   Show all the rooms in the home.
3. Color or paint your picture.

Now show your picture to the class.
Tell about the home you have made.
Tell what each room is for.

Petunia Takes a Trip

PART TWO

Far Away

I am going to fly up to the sky.

Using Words About Far Away Places

Name the things in the picture that make you think of far away places.
What can you see in a far away place?
How would you get there?
What would you do there?

Make a Story

Use words about far away places
to finish the story.

Sam went to see his grandpa in ____.
He traveled a long way in a ____.
On the way, he saw a ____.

As You Read

In this part of the book you will
read about people and animals who
go to far away places.
You will read about the things they
do there and the people and animals
they meet.

Keep a Reader's Log.
You can write things about far away
places that you know about.
Make notes in the log about what you
read.
If you find new words in the stories
you read, you can put them in the log.

Do You Ever Pretend?

I like to pretend sometimes.
Do you ever like to pretend?
What do you like to pretend?

I like to pretend that I am far away.
I pretend that I am millions and
millions of miles away.
Millions and millions of miles away is
out in space.
It is too far for me to go, but it is
fun to pretend to be there.

I think about things that took place
long ago.
Books can tell me about long ago, and
they can tell me about far away, too.

Do you ever find that reading helps
you to pretend?
Try reading about far away, or
long ago.
You will find out how much fun it is.

The Birds Take a Fall Trip

by Lewis L. Symonds

Many birds make a big trip south each fall.

When fall comes, they know that winter will soon be here.

They know that they have to find a warm place to stay for the winter.

They fly far away to the south, to a place where it stays warm.

Then, when winter is over, the birds fly back home again.

How do the birds know that winter is on the way?

In the fall, it is not as warm as it has been.

That is one way the birds can tell that they have to fly away to find a warm place.

The goose is one of the birds that has
to fly south each fall.
Sometimes you can see many geese
flying in the sky.

Look up at the sky on a fall day.
When geese fly, they look like a V.
The goose at the front of the V will
point the way for the birds that
fly with it.
Many birds fly like that.
Ducks fly in a V, too.
That way, the first duck can help point
the way south.

How do the birds find the way on this long trip?
What do they do if they lose the way?

One idea is that the birds look at the sun or the stars.
They know where the sun will come up each day and where it will go down when the day is over.
The sun may help birds find the way.
The stars may help, too.

Clouds may make a bird lose its way.
When many clouds are in the sky, the
birds can't see the sun.
Then the sun can't help the birds.

Some birds have to stop the trip when
there is rain.
They find a dry place, maybe a tree.
When the rain has stopped, they fly on.

The birds you see here are swallows.
It is fall, and the swallows have been
flying to a warm winter home in the
south.
Swallows fly by day.
When day is over, they find a place
to sleep.

The swallows have stopped in a big
tree to eat and sleep.
Each day when the sun is up, they
will fly on.
Then, when winter is over, they will
fly back home again.

Not all birds have to fly far away to warm places for the winter.
The birds you see here are some that can stay in one place all year.
They can find food.
Many people like to help the birds by putting seed out.

After You Read

Think

1. Why do many birds fly south in the winter?

2. What kind of weather is best for the trip south?

3. Why do ducks fly in a big V?

Share

What are some ideas about how birds find the way on the long trip?

Write

Write two sentences.
Tell two ways people can help birds that do not fly south in winter.

Read

You can read more about birds in "Song of the Swallows," by Leo Politi.

Sea Frog, City Frog

by Dorothy O. Van Woerkom

Sea Frog lived in a bog by the sea.
City Frog lived in a pond in the city.

One day when the sun was bright, Sea
Frog said, "I have been happy here,
but how nice it would be to see the
city!"

And City Frog said, "I would like to
see the sea!"

So City Frog jumped out of her pond.
She hopped down the road to the sea.

And Sea Frog jumped out of her bog.
She hopped up the road to the city.

The two frogs hopped for a day and
a night.
At last they came to a hill.

Up one side of the hill hopped City
Frog.
How tired she was!

Up the other side of the hill hopped
Sea Frog.
And she was tired!

The two frogs met at the top of the
hill.

"I am from the city," said City Frog.
"I am going to the sea.
Where are you from?
Where are you going?"

Sea Frog said, "I am from the sea, and
I am going to the city."

"How nice to see you," said City Frog.
"Let us stay and talk for a bit."

So they sat by the side of a big rock.
They talked.
They took a nap.

Then City Frog said, "I wish that we
were tall."

Sea Frog frowned.
"What good would that do?" she said.
"Would it get you to the sea, and me to the city?"

"No," said City Frog.
"But here we are on top of this hill.
Now, if we were tall, we could see far away.
Then we would not lose the way."

"How smart you are!" Sea Frog said.
"We can be tall."

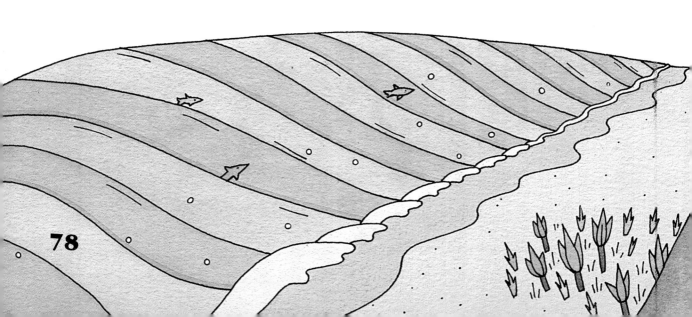

"Show me how we can do that," said
City Frog.

"Like this," said Sea Frog.
Sea Frog stood up on her long back
legs.
"We can be tall if we hold on to each
other!"

So the frogs stood on their long back
legs and held on to each other.
Their heads pointed up in the sky.

"When I hold on to you, I can see a
long way!" said City Frog.

"So can I," Sea Frog said.

So City Frog turned her nose to
the sea.
And Sea Frog turned her nose to
the city.
The noses of the frogs were turned
where they wanted to go.
But the eyes of the frogs were at the
back of the frogs' heads.
They just saw where they each had
come from!

"My!" said Sea Frog.
"The city is just like the sea!"

City Frog said, "The sea is just like the
city!"

So the frogs went home again.
The Sea Frog lived in the bog by
the sea.
The City Frog lived in the pond by
the city.
And they never ever saw that the sea
is not like the city, and the city is not
at all like the sea.

After You Read

Think

1. How did the City Frog and the Sea Frog meet?

2. Why did the frogs think that the city and the sea were the same?

3. Did the frogs find out what far away places are like?

Share

What are some ways to find out about far away places?

Write

Write two sentences.
Pretend that you are the Sea Frog.
Tell what you saw on the trip.

Read

You can read more about frogs in ''Big Boss,'' by Anne Rockwell.

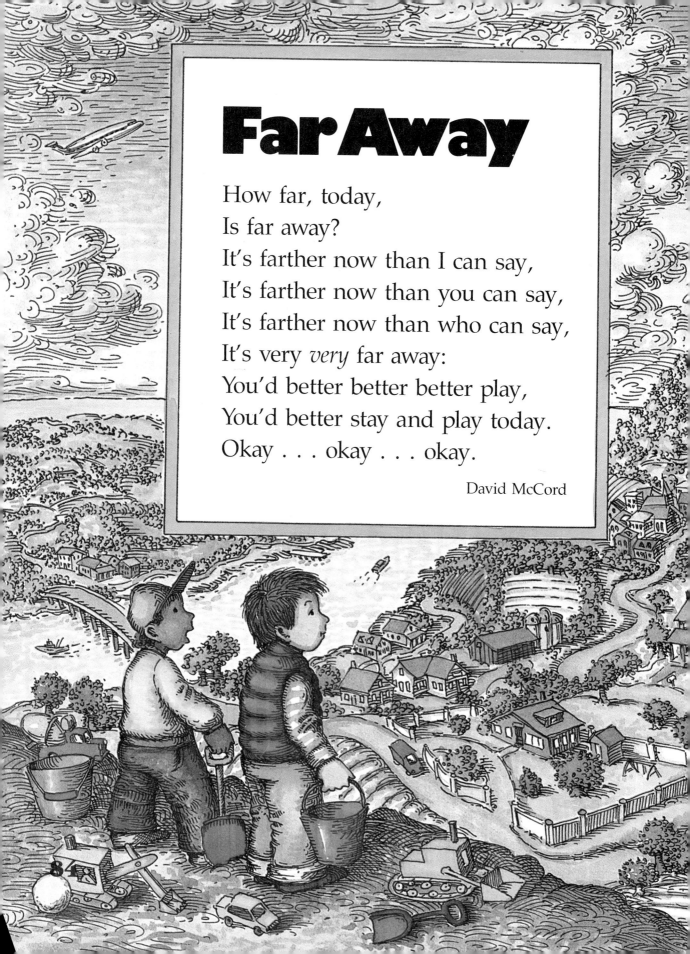

Far Away

How far, today,
Is far away?
It's farther now than I can say,
It's farther now than you can say,
It's farther now than who can say,
It's very *very* far away:
You'd better better better play,
You'd better stay and play today.
Okay . . . okay . . . okay.

David McCord

Understanding Fantasy

STRATEGY
◀BUILDER▶

for **Not THIS Bear** and **Fish Story**

Some stories tell about things
that could never really happen.
In these stories, animals and people
may do things that they can not do
in real life.

Thinking About Fantasy

A story that tells about things
that could never really happen is
called a fantasy.
In some fantasy stories, animals
may talk.
The people in fantasy stories may
fly or sit on clouds.
Fantasy stories are fun to read.

As You Read

Ask yourself: Could the things that
happen in the next two stories
happen in real life?

Use the words in blue to help you.

Not THIS Bear!

by Bernice Myers

Little Herman went to see his Aunt Gert.
He took the bus to the last stop.
But he still had a short walk to her house.

It was very cold.

And to keep warm, Herman pulled on his long furry coat.

And he pulled on his furry hat, which
came down over his head.

He looked just like a bear, which is
just what a bear thought he looked
like.

"You must be my cousin Julius!" said
the bear.
Grabbing Herman by the hand, the
bear ran with him to his cave.

A bear cannot
talk. Now you
know this is a
fantasy story.

"Look who I found in the woods!" the bear cried.

All the bears think that Herman is a bear.

All the bears ran to see Herman. "Cousin Julius, Cousin Julius!" they cried.

"My name is Herman," said Herman. But they did not hear him.

"I am not a bear . . . ," Herman said.

"Come and eat your soup," Mother Bear called.

When Mother Bear put out the soup,
all the bears lapped it up.

But Herman did not lap up his soup.
He ate soup with a spoon that he had
with him.
The bears had never seen a spoon.

"My, my!" Big Bear said, when
Herman was done eating.
"How clever you are to learn a trick
like that."

The bears smiled because they still thought that Herman was a bear.

Think about how Herman can show he is not a bear.

"I have to show that I am a boy," thought Herman.

He started to sing.
He stood on his head.
He did all the things a boy knows how to do.

But the bears just smiled at his tricks.

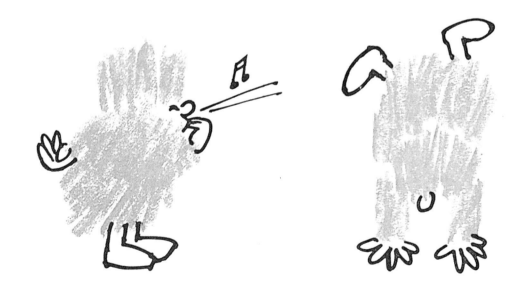

"See what can be done," said Dad,
"when a bear can go to the big city to learn."

"What a clever cousin we have," said
Big Bear.
And he yawned and went outside.

Big Bear looked at the sky and saw
what time of year it was—winter.

And so, all the bears got into their
beds to go to sleep.

Think about
what real bears
do in winter.

91

"We must sleep all winter," said Big
Bear.

"All winter!" said Herman.
"I sleep just one night at a time.
In the day I go out and play.
I am NOT sleeping all winter!"

"But all bears do," said a baby bear.

This is funny
because
Herman is not a
bear.

"Not THIS bear," said Herman.
"I like winter."

"He likes winter," said the bears with
surprise.

"Yes, I like winter.
I like to play in the snow with my
friends.
And, I have to go to school."

When Herman was done, no one said
a thing.

Then Big Bear frowned and said,
"Maybe you aren't a bear."

Think about
what will
happen next.

"Look!" cried a bear.
She took Herman's furry hat and
coat.
"He is not a bear at all."

The bears now
know that
Herman is not
really a bear.

And there stood little Herman.

Dad Bear thought that was good fun.

"That is the most clever trick of all,"
he said.
"And the trick was on us."

94

Herman put on his furry hat and coat
again.
He said goodbye to all the bears.

Think about
where Herman
will go next.

"It has been nice to have you with us.
Come and see us when winter ends,"
they said with a yawn.

"I will," he said.

And Herman started to walk in the
snow to his Aunt Gert's house.
He didn't want to lose his way.

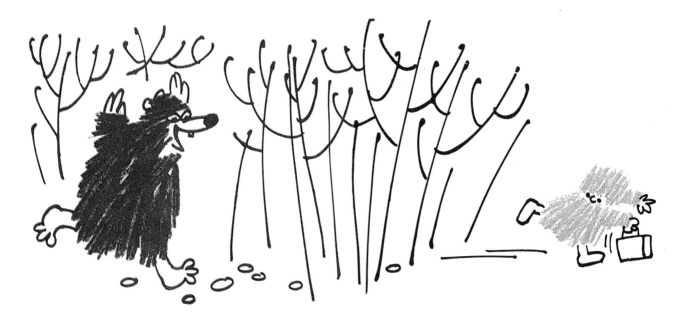

He was just out of the woods when a
big black bear jumped out.
He ran to Herman and cried, "Cousin
Bernard!"

Think about why
Herman ran so
fast.
But Herman ran just as fast as he
could.

Herman was glad, when at last, he
reached Aunt Gert's porch.

Aunt Gert was very glad to see
Herman.

After You Read

Think

1. Why did the bears think that Herman was a bear?

2. What did the bears think of Herman eating with a spoon?

3. How did Herman show the bears that he was not a bear?

Share

What other things could Herman have done to show that he was not a bear?

Write

Write a sentence about a place you would like to visit.

Read

"Seven True Bear Stories," by Laura Geringer, is about real bears.

Fish Story

by Robert Tallon

Long ago, a clever fish lived in a
pretty lake.
"I have to get out of here!" Little Fish
said.
"I am tired of swimming in the same
water.
I want a bigger pond."

Big Cat was walking by just then.

"I want to see the world," Little Fish
said to the hungry Big Cat.

"The world is wonderful up here, just
wonderful," Big Cat said.

"Old Fish told me about the world
and the sea," Little Fish said.
"Please, can you take me to the sea?"

"Yes I can," said Big Cat.
He picked up Little Fish.
He put Little Fish in a bag.

"Thank you so much," Little Fish said.

"I am glad to help a friend," said Big Cat, as he ran into the woods.

"How pretty . . . is that a tree?" Little Fish asked.

"Yes, that is a tree," said Big Cat.

"Could we stop and look at the other pretty trees?" Little Fish asked.

"No!" Big Cat yelled.

"Where is the sea?" Little Fish asked.

"Just over the hill," Big Cat said. "Now stop talking."

"But the world is so new to me," Little Fish said.

Big Cat ran into a little house.

"Is the sea in here?" Little Fish asked.

"Your trip is over," Big Cat said.

Little Fish looked around at the pots and pans in the room.

"Is . . . is . . . this your pond?" he asked.

"It is my house, Fish," Big Cat said. "I am hungry, and I am going to eat you!"

"Why me?" Little Fish asked.

Big Cat sang as he picked up a pot. He was very loud. "Didn't Old Fish tell you about cats and fishes?" he asked.

"Are you a CAT?" Little Fish asked.

"Yes, Big Cat is the name. And I am going to eat you!"

"But I am all bones," Little Fish cried.

"Stop talking, I am trying to read this book," Big Cat said.

"Yes, here it is . . . I will bake you!
And when I am done cooking, I will
eat you!"

"Big Cat, wait, please!" Little Fish
cried, as loud as he could.
"I am all bones, but I know a big
fish . . . much bigger than me!
If you take me back to the lake, I will
get this pretty fish for you."

"How?" Big Cat asked.

"Have you got some ketchup?" Little
Fish asked.

"What if I do?" Big Cat asked.

"This fish likes ketchup very much
and he is hungry," Little Fish said.
"Just take me back and I will tie a rope
around the big fish.
Bring a rope, some ketchup, and leave
the rest to me."

Big Cat took up Little Fish, the
ketchup, and a rope and raced back to
the pond.
He put Little Fish into the pond.
He put in the rope with the ketchup.
Little Fish swam into the pond.

"Thank you, Big Cat.
How wonderful to be back in my
pretty pond," he said as he swam
around and around.
Big Cat pulled on the rope a little.
"Little Fish, get your big friend.
I am hungry now!" he said.

Little Fish tied the rope to an old bike.
"Pull it up!" Little Fish called.
Big Cat pulled on the rope.
He pulled out the old bike!

"It was a trick!" Big Cat yelled.

Little Fish smiled as he swam away.
"It was just a Fish Story," he sang.
"Just a Fish Story . . . for a Big Cat!"

After You Read

Think

1. Why did Little Fish ask Big Cat for help?

2. What did Big Cat have planned for Little Fish?

3. How did Little Fish trick Big Cat?

Share

What would be a good, safe way that Little Fish could get out of his pond and see the world.

Write

Write a sentence.
Tell what it was that Little Fish did not know about Big Cat.

Read

"Harriet and the Garden," by Nancy Carlson, is another book about animals.

Meet Robert Tallon

Robert Tallon wrote "Fish Story." He painted the funny pictures, too.

Mr. Tallon has always liked to write, to draw, and to paint. He had many happy times when he was a boy. His mom and dad liked to tell funny stories. They liked to read the funny stories he wrote, too. Mr. Tallon thinks this helped him grow up to write funny books.

Mr. Tallon wrote about animals in "Fish Story," "Flea Story," and "Worm Story." He wrote about funny monsters in the books "The Thing in Delores' Piano" and "Zoophabets."

MAKING ALL THE
CONNECTIONS

Talk About Far Away Places

Look at the picture.
Think about all the far away places
in the stories.
Where did the people and animals
go in the stories?
What did they do there?
Which place did you like the best?

The Birds Take a Fall Trip

Sea Frog, City Frog

Not THIS Bear!

Fish Story

Read Something New

This is a letter that Maria wrote
when her friend Jill moved far away.

Dear Jill,
I miss you now that you have
moved away.
Please tell me about your
new home.
Do you like it?
        Your friend,
         Maria

Now read what Jill wrote back.

Dear Maria,
My new home is nice.
There is a lake by my house.
Can you come and see
me soon?
        Your friend,
           Jill

What did Maria want Jill to do?
How did Jill do it?

MAKING ALL THE CONNECTIONS

Think About the Stories

Letters are one good way to talk to someone who is far away.
Here are some people, animals and places from the stories.
Use the words in the box to tell who they might send letters to.

the bears	pond
Jill	City Frog

1. Maria sent a letter to _____.
2. Little Fish might send a letter to his friends in the _____.
3. Sea Frog might send a letter to _____.
4. Herman might send a thank-you letter to _____.

The first sentence is about Maria.
Why did Maria send a letter?
What did Maria say in her letter?
Now it is time for you to write a letter.

Write a Letter

A letter is a way you can talk to someone who is far away.

Plan   Think of someone to write to. Think of something to ask about the far away place.
Think of something you want to tell.

Write   Now you can write your letter. Look back at the letters Maria and Jill wrote and find the parts of a letter.
- ◆ Start by writing: Dear (name),
- ◆ Then write what you want to say.
- ◆ End by writing: Your friend,

  (your name)

Check   Can you read your letter? Did you ask about a far away place? Did you tell about something, too? Did you end each sentence with an end mark . or ?

Share   Now you can send your letter.

Nicolas,
Where Have
You Been?

PART THREE

Learning

What do little mice eat?

Using Words About Learning

Think of all the things you know how to do.

Most of those things had to be learned.

Look at the picture.

What things have people learned to do?

What new things would you like to learn?

116

Make a Story

Use words about learning how to do
things to finish the story.

Fran wanted to ____ how to ride a bike.
Dad helped Fran by ____.
Fran did what Dad said and soon
she ____.

As You Read
In this part of the book you will read
about learning.
You will read about how people
learn about the world.
You will read about some animals
who learn new things.

Keep a Reader's Log.
You can write words about learning
and doing new things in it.
Make notes in the log about what you
read.
If you find new words in the stories
you read, you can put them in the log.

It Is Easy To Learn

There was a time when it wasn't easy for me to learn things.
I learned how to learn by studying the floor of the sea.
I wanted to understand how things live there.

First, I looked for books to read about the floor of the sea.
Some were easy to find, but some I had to search for in the library.
I learned how to find books in the library.

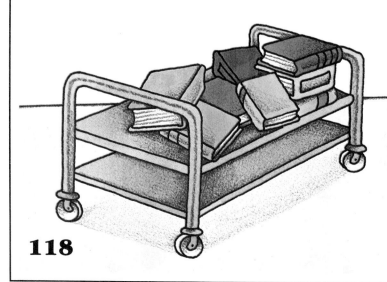

Then, I had to search in the books
for the parts about the floor of the sea.
I had to find the parts that would tell
me how things can live there.
Reading books helped me understand
the floor of the sea.

Then, I started to understand about
learning, too.
Learning is knowing how to search
for things.
I understand how to search for
things now.

What Will the Weather Be?

by Stanley Elvin

Can you tell what the weather will be?

Some people think that they can.

These people look at plants and animals to find out about the weather.

Sometimes people look at birds to tell the weather.

When people see a few birds flying high, far from shore, people think that it will be a nice day.

This is because birds don't like to
fly out to sea if they think there
is going to be a storm.
When the weather is going to be bad,
sea birds stay near shore.

A strong wind can come with a storm.
Birds don't like to fly in a strong
wind.
They sit in a tree when they think
that rain or a strong wind is
on the way.

People in the country have a few different ways to tell what the weather will be.
Some people in the country look at different farm animals.
A chicken may make a loud clucking sound when rain is on the way.
The chicken might jump off its nest and run around and around.

Sheep on a farm can show when it will be cold, too.
Sheep will stand close together when it is going to be cold.

Some people say that different wild animals can show when the weather will be cold.
If it is going to be a cold winter, wild animals will make better, warmer nests in the fall.

Wild animals who live in high hills in the country can show the weather, too.
If they come down off the hills, bad winter weather is on the way.
This is because it gets colder up in the hills.

123

A frog can show the weather, too.
A tree frog will croak louder when
rain is on the way.
It will stay down in the water.
On a nice day, a tree frog will not
make a loud croaking sound.
It will come out of the water and go
high up in the trees.
These are a few of the ways that
wild animals tell people about the
weather.

Plants tell people about the weather, too.
Plants get cold in winter weather. When it gets very cold, each leaf of this plant will turn in.

People need to know what the weather will be.

People in the country look at different animals and plants to find out about the weather.

These people look at these animals and plants to find out when it will rain, when it will be cold, and when it will be nice.

After You Read

Think

1. What are some ways that sea birds can show what the weather will be?

2. How can you tell the weather by looking at wild animals?

3. How can people in the country tell what the weather will be?

Share

What are some more ways that we can find out what the weather will be?

Write

Draw a bird in a storm.
Then draw a bird on a nice day.

Read

Read more about weather in "Gilberto and the Wind," by Mary Hall Ets.

Down the Hill

by Arnold Lobel

Frog went to Toad's house.

"Toad, wake up," he cried.
"Come out and see how great the
winter is!"

"I will not," said Toad.
"I am in my warm bed."

"Winter is great," said Frog.
"Come out and have fun."

"No," said Toad.
"I have no winter clothes."

Frog came into the house.
"I have some clothes for you to put
on," he said.

Frog pulled a coat down over the top
of Toad.
Frog pulled pants up over Toad's
feet and legs.
He put a hat upon Toad's head.

"Help!" cried Toad.
"My best friend is trying to kill me
with a coat, pants, and a hat!"

"I am just getting you ready for
winter," laughed Frog.

Frog and Toad went out.
They tramped in the snow.

"We will ride down this big hill
upon my sled," said Frog.

"Not me," said Toad.

"Do not be afraid," said Frog.
"I will be with you on the sled.
It will be a fine, fast ride.
Toad, you sit in front.
I will sit right behind you."

Frog sat behind Toad on the sled.
The sled moved down the hill.

"Are you ready?
Here we go!" said Frog.

There was a bump.
Frog fell off the sled.
Toad rushed past trees and rocks.

"Frog, I am glad that you are here,"
said Toad.
"I would not like to be by myself."

Toad leaped over a hill of snow.
"I could not drive the sled without
you behind me," said Toad.
"You are right.
Winter is great!" he laughed.

A bird was flying by.

"Look at Frog and me," called Toad.
"We can ride a sled better than
everyone in the world!"

"But Toad," said the bird.
"Frog is not on the sled."

Toad looked behind him.
He saw that Frog was not there.

"I AM ALL BY MYSELF!" cried Toad.

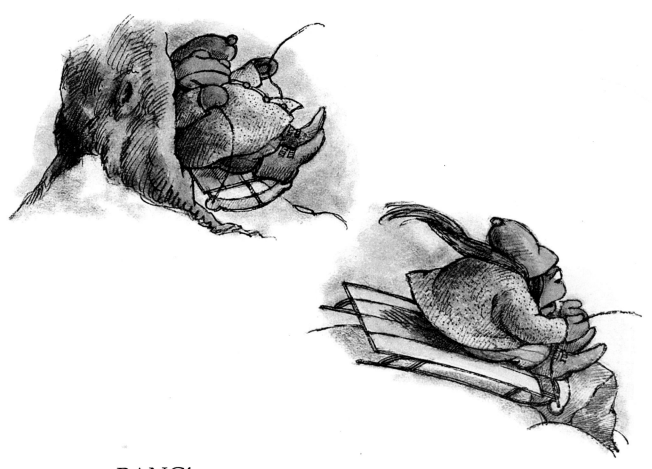

BANG!
The sled hit a tree.

THUD!
The sled hit a rock.

PLOP!
The sled went right into the snow.

Frog came running down the hill.
He pulled Toad out of the snow.

"I saw everything," said Frog.
"You did very well without me."

"I did not," said Toad.
"But there is one thing that I am
ready to do all by myself."

"What is that?" asked Frog.

"I can go home by myself," said Toad.
"I quit.
It may be true that winter is great,
but bed is better."

After You Read

Think

1. What do Frog and Toad think about winter?

2. Can Toad ride a sled well?

3. Why do you think Toad likes the sled ride at first, but not at the end?

Share

What did Toad learn about winter?

Write

Write a list.
List the things you like to do best in winter.

Read

You can read more about winter in "The Snowy Day," by Ezra Jack Keats.

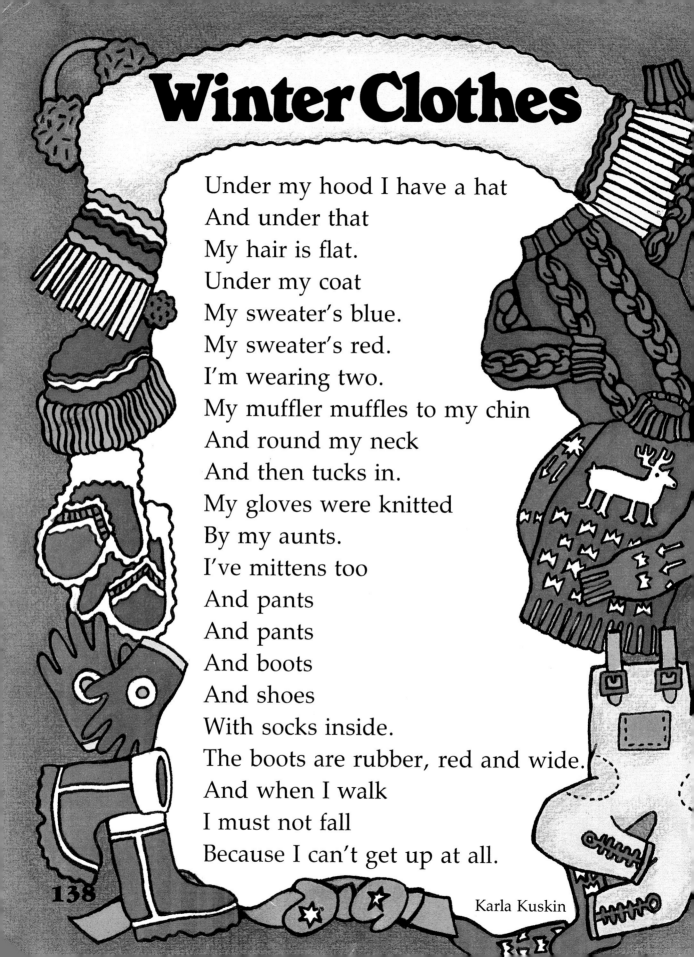

Winter Clothes

Under my hood I have a hat
And under that
My hair is flat.
Under my coat
My sweater's blue.
My sweater's red.
I'm wearing two.
My muffler muffles to my chin
And round my neck
And then tucks in.
My gloves were knitted
By my aunts.
I've mittens too
And pants
And pants
And boots
And shoes
With socks inside.
The boots are rubber, red and wide.
And when I walk
I must not fall
Because I can't get up at all.

Karla Kuskin

Guessing What Will Happen

What will happen next?

Thinking About What Will Happen

As you read a story, you can try to guess how it will end.

You can use what you already know to guess how it will end.

You know that the animal in the picture likes to eat nuts.

This helps you guess that the animal will eat the nuts.

As You Read

Ask yourself: What do I know that helps me guess how the next two stories will end?

Use the words in blue to help you.

The Ant and the Dove

by Daniel Lewis

An ant was going by a nice clean river.

Think about how the ant could get the water.

"I want a drink of water," she said.
"I will get a drink from the river.
How am I going to get down there from up here?
How am I going to get to the water for a drink?"

Then the ant saw a tall blade of
grass.
"That is how I will get a drink of
water," she said.
"I will go down that tall blade of
grass.
Yes, that is a good idea."

Going down the blade of grass was
not a good idea.
On the way down, the ant fell into
the water.

Guess what the
ant will do with
the blade of
grass.

"Help! Help!" said the ant.
"I fell into the river and I can't
swim."

There was a tree by the river.
A pretty dove was in the tree.
The dove saw the ant in the water.
She saw that the ant could not swim.

Think about
what the dove
will do.

The dove looked for a way to help
the ant.
Then she saw a big green leaf.

142

The dove got the leaf with her bill.
She let the leaf drop into the water.

"Get on the leaf," the dove said to
the ant.
"The leaf will bring you to the
shore."

The ant did just what the dove said
to do.
Soon the ant was on the shore.

Think about
what will
happen to the
dove.

Just then a man came to the river.
He had come to the river to catch
a dove to take home and keep
in a cage.
The man saw the dove.
The dove did not see the man.

The man did catch the dove.
He put the pretty dove in the cage.
She beat her wings on the bars of
the cage, trying to get out.

144

"Help! Help!" said the dove.
"This man wants to catch me and keep
me in this cage."

Guess who will help the dove.

"Do not beat your wings.
I am going to bite the man.
When I bite him, he will drop the
cage," said the ant.
"Then the cage will break open and
you can fly away."

The ant bit the man in the leg.
The man dropped the cage and it did
break open.

When the dove saw that the cage did
break open, she said with joy, "It
was good of you to help me.
I didn't want that man to catch me."

The ant said, "When I fell into the
water, you helped me.
From this day on, I will try to be
good to those who are good to me."

"That is true," said the dove.
"It is best that no one forgets to
be good."

After You Read

Think

1. Why did the ant need help?

2. How did the dove help the ant?

3. What did the dove and the ant learn about helping?

Share

Did you guess that the ant would help the dove?

Write

Write two sentences.
Tell how you can help someone who has helped you.

Read

"Andy and the Lion," by James Daugherty, tells about two more friends who help each other.

Just the Thing for Geraldine

A play from a book
by Ellen Conford

CAST

NARRATOR	FATHER
GERALDINE	RANDOLPH
MOTHER	EUGENE

NARRATOR: Geraldine loved to juggle
things.
Her mother and father thought
she juggled too much.
So they gave her five cents and
sent her to a dance class.

MOTHER: Dance class will help you to grow.

FATHER: It will help you to dance better.

RANDOLPH: It will help keep you fit.

EUGENE: Nothing can help her.

NARRATOR: So Geraldine went to dance class.
She came home very happy.

GERALDINE: Everyone, come look!
Come look at what I can do!

NARRATOR: Geraldine lifted her
hands and danced around the
tree, singing with joy.

MOTHER: How wonderful!

FATHER: Again! Again!

RANDOLPH: That isn't bad at all.

EUGENE: Can I go play now?

NARRATOR: All at once Geraldine fell on the floor.

MOTHER: Geraldine! Are you hurt?

GERALDINE: No, I feel fine.

FATHER: Don't laugh, Randolph.

RANDOLPH: (laughing) I tried not to.

EUGENE: Do you care if I laugh?

NARRATOR: The next day, Geraldine
was very sad when she came
home from dance class.

MOTHER: Well, what did you learn in
dance class today?

GERALDINE: I learned that I can't dance.
I tried, but I can't bend my legs
and I always fall on the floor and
get hurt.
I don't feel like going back.
I quit.

NARRATOR: So, Geraldine's mother and father gave her five cents and told her to choose another class.

On the third day, Geraldine came home carrying something in wet leaves.

RANDOLPH: What is that?

GERALDINE: It is clay.

I have to make it look like someone for my class.

EUGENE: That sounds like fun!
Choose me, Geraldine!

GERALDINE: I will, but you have to sit
very still.

NARRATOR: So Geraldine tried to
make the clay look like her
brother Eugene.
She tried for a long time . . .

EUGENE: Can't I go yet?

GERALDINE: No, I am still working.

NARRATOR: At last Geraldine stopped
working on the clay.
She put leaves all around it.

EUGENE: Why are you doing that?
I can't see what it looks like!

GERALDINE: I don't want you to see it
yet because it is not ready.
Get your hands off it!

EUGENE: I will not break it.
I just want to see it!

NARRATOR: Geraldine's mother and father and brother Randolph came running.

FATHER: What is going on?

MOTHER: Why are you two yelling?

RANDOLPH: What is that strange thing?

GERALDINE: Eugene, stop pulling off the leaves!
I don't want you to open it yet.

NARRATOR: But it was too late.
Her brother Eugene had pulled
off all the leaves.
Eugene was not at all happy.

EUGENE: That is not me!
That is a lot of bumps!
Do I look like a lot of
bumps?

GERALDINE: (in a sad way) No, you
don't look like that.
I will put the leaves back on top
of it.

NARRATOR: When she was done,
Geraldine went off to another
tree.
She stayed there and juggled.
After a time, her brothers came
and sat down next to her.

RANDOLPH: Boy, do you juggle well,
Geraldine.

GERALDINE: Thank you.

EUGENE: Yes, boy, I wish I could
juggle like you can, Geraldine.

RANDOLPH: There is no one who can juggle better than you can. ISN'T THAT RIGHT, EUGENE?

EUGENE: Right.

RANDOLPH: We want you to show us how to juggle, DON'T WE?

EUGENE: Yes.

GERALDINE: Well, it isn't hard to learn to juggle. Here, let me show you how . . .

159

NARRATOR: Just then, Geraldine's mother and father came up to the tree.

MOTHER: Geraldine, I have a third class you could go to . . .

GERALDINE: (laughing) I have a better idea.
I am going to GIVE a class.
I will show everyone how to juggle, and they will have to give me SIX cents a class.

After You Read

Think

1. Why did everyone want Geraldine to take a class?

2. How did Geraldine feel after her two classes?

3. What did Geraldine do best?

Share

Is there something that you can do well that you could show someone how to do?

Write

Write one sentence.
Tell how you feel when you do something well.

Read

Read more plays in ''Small Plays for Special Days,'' by Sue Alexander.

MAKING ALL THE
CONNECTIONS

Talk About It

Look at the picture.
Think about the stories in this part of
the book.
Think about the people and animals
in the stories.
What did they learn?
How did they learn it?
Who do you think learned the most?

What Will the Weather Be?
Down the Hill
The Ant and the Dove
Just the Thing for Geraldine

Make an Animal Mask

People like to learn about animals.
People also like to learn how to make things.
You can learn about an animal and make an animal mask.

1. Pick an animal to learn about.
2. Use books and pictures to find out things about the animal.
3. Draw the animal's face on a piece of paper.
4. Cut out the face and color it in.
5. Make holes so that you can see.
6. Tape string to the sides of the mask and tie it around your head.
7. Wear your mask and tell the class what you learned about the animal.

Pig Pig Grows Up

PART FOUR

Growing

You are a big pig now, Pig Pig.

Using Words About Growing

Look at the picture.
What things in the picture will grow?
Can you think of other things that grow?
Can you think of something that grows very big?

Make a Story

Use words about growing to finish the story.

Pat was getting _____.
She could now _____.
People said she looked _____.

As You Read

In this part of the book you will read about things that grow.
You will read about how plants, animals, and people grow.
You will read about how plants, animals and people change as they grow.

Keep a Reader's Log.
You can write words about growing that you know.
Make notes in the log about what you read.
If you find new words in the stories you read, you can put them in the log.

I Am Growing

I have noticed something very
wonderful about myself.
I have noticed that I am growing.
Have you noticed that?
Did you know that you are growing?

Growing is not something that
is fast.
You grow very slowly.
But before you know it, you are
growing up.
It seems like magic.

Some things take a long time to grow.
It may seem to you that you are
growing very slowly, but some trees
grow much more slowly.
When a thing grows so very slowly,
you might think that it is not growing
at all.
But look at a tree.
See how tall a tree is.
No one noticed that tree growing, but
now it is big.
That is the magic of growing.

A Nest of Wood Ducks

by Evelyn Shaw

On a little lake in the forest,
a pair of birds swims side by side.
They are a pair of wood ducks.
The mother wood duck is called a hen.

The hen flaps her wings and
goes up into a tree in the forest.
There is a small hole in the trunk of
the tree.
Inside the hole it is dark.
Her nest is here.
Six eggs are in the nest.

Now the hen will stay in the nest.
For many days she will sit on the
eggs to keep them warm.
Inside the eggs the baby ducks are
starting to grow.
The hen sits on her eggs most of
the day and all of the night.

Days pass by.
A baby duck is growing inside each egg.
The baby ducks are ready at last
to come out of their eggs.

One baby duck starts to crack
open its shell.
More baby ducks crack their shells.
Before long, all the baby ducks
climb out of their eggs.
At first, they are wet and not
very strong.
After a while, they are hopping
around their mother.

The next day, the baby ducks call
to each other and jump up and down.
They are ready to leave the nest.
They are ready to swim and find food.

The hen dives down to the lake.
The baby ducks hop up and down.
One baby duck climbs to the top of
the hole.
It does not want to go.
Then it opens its wings and goes
down into the water.
Then all the baby ducks climb to
the hole and jump down.
Each one swims to the hen.

Now the hen and the baby ducks
will live on the lake.
The hen will take care of the
baby ducks.

The baby ducks learn to chase
bugs for food.
At first, the baby ducks do not
get the bugs.
They try again and again.
At last, they are fast and can
catch them.
The baby ducks eat seeds, too.

The baby ducks hide from animals
that may try to eat them.
On the lake they dive under the water.
On land they hide in the weeds
and do not move.

Days pass by.
The ducks are growing bigger.
Their wings grow strong.

Now the hen does not need to take
care of them.
They can fly.

Before long they join the other wood
ducks and fly away for the winter.
So does the hen.

The next year a pair of wood ducks
goes to the forest by the lake.
The pair of wood ducks is looking
for a nest in the forest.

The hen climbs into holes in trees.
There is an old nest in one hole.
The hen chooses this place for her
nest.

The hen does not know that once
she lived in this same hole.
She was a baby duck here.
It is the nest that her mother made
last year.

176

After You Read

Think

1. What kind of place do wood ducks need for a nest?

2. Where do wood ducks live?

3. What do baby wood ducks learn to do to stay safe?

Share

Why would staying very still keep the baby ducks safe?

Write

The baby ducks had to work hard.
Write a sentence.
Tell about something that you did that took hard work.

Read

''How Puppies Grow,'' by Millicent E. Selsam, tells how puppies grow up.

City Magic

by Laura Schenone
and Pat Garbarini

I want a pet very, very much.
My mother says I have to wait.
We have had this talk many times,
my mother and I.
Dad says I can buy some fish.
They are small and can fit well in
my small room.
But my brother has four fish.
I want something different.
I want something of my own.

One day, Grandma showed me
flowers hanging in her window.
She had many kinds of flowers.
Grandma told me she would help me
grow flowers of my own.
She said that they are not the same
as a pet, but that flowers can
bring magic to a city home.

Grandma took me to buy some flower
seeds and told me what to do.
Now I have all kinds of flowers
hanging in the window of my room.
I still want a pet, but a window
full of flowers is nice, too.

How to Grow a Flower

There are many different kinds
of flowers that are easy to grow.
Most flowers can be started as seeds.
Here is an easy way to grow a flower
from a seed.

To grow a flower, you will need
to do these things:

◆ buy your seeds
◆ buy or make a pot
◆ get some soil
◆ get three or four small rocks
◆ get some water.

1. Get a small pot for your flower.
   You can use a can for a pot.
   Clean the can out very well.
   Get someone to help you make
   three or four small holes in the
   end of the can.

2. Put the rocks in the pot.
   They will help to keep the soil
   from being too wet.

3. Fill the pot with soil so that
   it is not quite full.

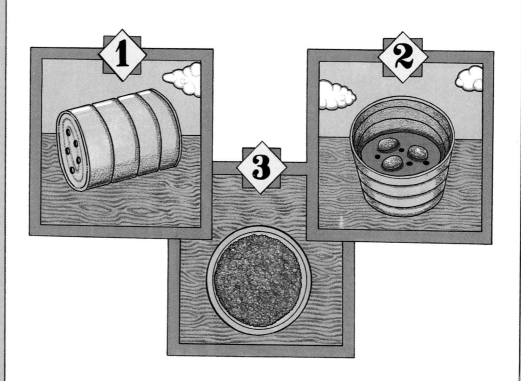

4. Dig three or four small holes
in the soil.
Drop a seed in each hole.
Pat some soil down over the seeds.

5. Water the soil with care.
Use a dish under the pot to catch
the water.
As you water it, look for the water
to drop from the holes in the end
of the pot.
When it starts to drop, the seeds
have all the water they need.

6. Put the pot and dish near
   a window where there is sun.

7. Feel the soil each day.
   If it is not wet, water it a bit.
   Now it is time to wait.
   The seeds will grow slowly.

8. After many days, you will see
   small green plants in your pot.
   Keep waiting and watering.
   Before long, you will have flowers
   that you helped to grow.

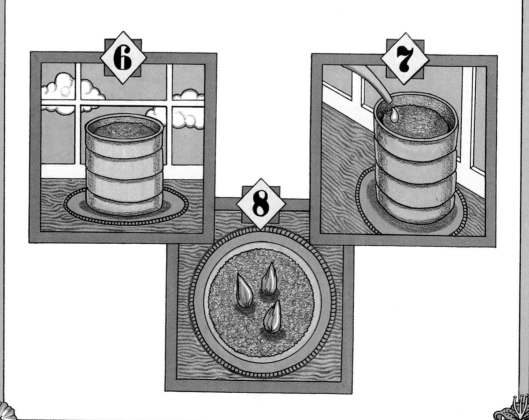

After You Read

Think

1. What was Grandma's idea for something to care for?

2. What do you think about before you try to grow a plant?

3. What is the best place for a plant that grows in a pot?

Share

How are pets and plants different?

Write

Write a sentence.
Tell why you think this story is called ''City Magic.''

Read

''A Garden for Miss Mouse,'' by Michaela Muntean, is another book about plants.

Maytime
Magic

A little seed
For me to sow . . .

A little earth
To make it grow . . .
A little hole,
A little pat . . .
A little wish,
And that is that.

A little sun,
A little shower . . .
A little while,
And then—a flower!

Mabel Watts

Understanding Folk Tales

Folk tales are stories that were
made up a long time ago.
Folk tales may be about animals or
people.

Thinking About Folk Tales

Animals may act like people in folk
tales.
Sometimes the animals may try to
trick each other.
In folk tales, there may be people
who do silly things, too.
Many times, the things that happen
in folk tales are funny.

As You Read

Ask yourself: What is funny about the
next two folk tales?

Use the words in blue to help you.

The Turnip

by Michael Patrick Hearn

Think about what the man wants.

One day, a man planted a turnip seed.
He planned to grow a turnip that
would win a prize and make him rich.
He waited and waited for it to grow.
Then the time came to pull it out.

"This turnip will win the prize.
I will be rich," the man said.

The man took hold of the turnip.
He pulled and he pulled, but he
could not pull it out.

So the man called the woman.
"Help me pull out our turnip," the
man said.

Now two people
pull the turnip.

The woman pulled the man and the
man pulled the turnip.
They pulled and they pulled, but
they could not pull it out.

The woman called the boy.
"Help us pull out our turnip," the
woman said.

The boy pulled the woman.
The woman pulled the man and the
man pulled the turnip.
They pulled and they pulled, but
they could not pull it out.

Look at how the
word **pulled** is
used again and
again.

The boy called the girl.
"Help the three of us pull out our
turnip," the boy said.

Think about
what will
happen next.

The girl pulled the boy and the boy
pulled the woman.
The woman pulled the man
and the man pulled the turnip.
They pulled and they pulled, but they
could not pull it out.

192

The girl called the dog.
"Help us pull out our turnip," the
girl said.

The dog pulled the girl.
The girl pulled the boy and the boy
pulled the woman.
The woman pulled the man and the
man pulled the turnip.
They pulled and they pulled, but
they could not pull it out.

The dog called the cat.
"Help us pull out our turnip," the
dog said.

The cat pulled the dog and the
dog pulled the girl.
The girl pulled the boy and the boy
pulled the woman.
The woman pulled the man and the
man pulled the turnip.
They pulled and they pulled, but
they could not pull it out.

The cat called the mouse.
"Help us pull out our turnip," the
cat said.

The mouse pulled the cat.
The cat pulled the dog and the dog
pulled the girl.
The girl pulled the boy and the boy
pulled the woman.
The woman pulled the man and the man
pulled the turnip.
They pulled and they pulled and
they pulled.

Think about
what it will take
to get the turnip
out.

This ending is a
funny surprise.

Pop!
Out popped the turnip!

196 -

After You Read

Think

1. Why do you think it was hard to pull out the turnip?

2. What did it take to pull out the turnip at last?

3. How do you think the turnip got so big?

Share

What do you think would have happened if the mouse had not come to help?

Write

It took hard work to pull the turnip.
Make a list.
List in order who came to help.

Read

"Momotaro," by Robert Goodman, is another folk tale you might like.

Farming

by Betty Baker

Coyote liked melons, all kinds
of melons.
But he did not have any.

Badger had a farm.
Coyote went to Badger and said,
"We are partners.
We should farm together."

"All right," said Badger,
"Help me dig."

"No," said Coyote.
"I am not good at digging.
You are.
You dig.
I will do the planting."

"No," said Badger.
"If you plant, you will make a mess.
I will dig and plant.
You pull the weeds."

199

Coyote said, "A partner should make things easy for you.
You live in a hole, so you take everything that grows under the ground.
I will just keep what grows on top."

"All right," said Badger, and started to dig.
Coyote put his tail up and went away laughing.

When it was time to pull weeds,
Coyote was making a new song.
Badger pulled the weeds.

When it was time to pull them again,
Coyote was singing his new song to
the full moon.
Badger pulled the weeds.

Then Coyote went away to hunt
rabbits.

Badger pulled all the weeds.

When it was time to eat melons,
Coyote came back.
The plants were big and green.
But they had no melons.

"You took my melons!" said Coyote.
"You only get what grows under the ground.
Give me my melons."

Badger said, "You did not tell
me you wanted melons.
I planted what I always plant."

"What is that?" said Coyote.

"Potatoes," said Badger.
And he dug them up and ate them
all winter.

Coyote said, "It is not right for
one partner to get everything."

Badger said, "It is not right
for one partner to do everything."

"You are right," said Coyote.
"You dig and plant.
I will pull the weeds.
And this time, I will take what
grows under the ground."

"All right," said Badger, and he
started to dig.
Coyote put his tail up and went away
laughing.

And he did not come back until
it was time to eat potatoes.
The plants were big and green.
Coyote dug and dug.
But the plants had no potatoes.
"Where are my potatoes?" said
Coyote.

Badger said, "You did not tell me
you wanted potatoes.
Last time, you wanted melons.
So that is what I planted."

And he dried the melons and ate
them all winter.

After You Read

Think

1. How did Coyote try to trick Badger?

2. How did Badger trick Coyote?

3. Why didn't Coyote help as he had promised?

Share

What are some good ways to get people to work with each other to get something done?

Write

Write two sentences.
Tell when it is good to make a promise.

Read

Another folk tale about animals who play tricks is ''The Banza,'' by Diane Wolkstein.

MAKING ALL THE
CONNECTIONS

Talk About Growing

Look at the picture.
Think about the things that grow in
the stories.
How did they grow?
Think about the stories.
Which story did you like the best?

A NEST OF WOOD DUCKS

CITY MAGIC

THE TURNIP

FARMING

Read Something New

Jane wrote a book report about
"Pig Pig Grows Up."
Read what she wrote.

Title: Pig Pig Grows Up
Author: David McPhail

This book is about a pig.
He does not want to grow up.
I liked the book.
It was funny.
Pig Pig learns something.

What did Jane say about "Pig Pig
Grows Up"?
Did she like the book?

MAKING ALL THE CONNECTIONS

Think About the Stories

Finish the sentences about the stories in this part of the book.

1. Jane wrote a book report about ____.

2. "A Nest of Wood Ducks" tells how some ____ grow up.

3. "City Magic" tells you how to grow a ____.

4. "Farming" is about ____ and ____.

Each sentence tells something about the stories.
But they do not say how you feel about the stories.
Jane wrote a book report.
The report tells what the book is about.
It also tells how Jane feels about the book.
Now it is time for you to read a book and to write how you feel about it.

Write a Book Report

A book report tells about a book.
Now you can write a book report.

Plan Choose a book and read it.
Take notes about what happens in
the book.
Take notes about how you feel about
the book.

Write Now, write your book report.
1. Write the name of the book.
   This is the **title**.
2. Write down who wrote the book.
   This is the **author**.
3. Tell what or who the book is about.
4. Tell your feelings about the book.

Check Can you read your book report?
Did you use capital letters to start
the title and the name of the author?

Share You can read your book report
to the rest of the class.

Read the sentences.
Look at the pictures.
They will help you understand the words in dark print.

<u>Aa</u>

animal   A lion is a big **animal**.

<u>Bb</u>

badger   A **badger** lives in a hole in the ground.

blanket   The **blanket** on my bed is red.

bug   A **bug** is small and has many legs.

Cc

chair   You can sit on a **chair**.

coyote   The **coyote** looks like a wild dog.

Dd

dance   I will **dance** to the tune.

dove   A **dove** is a small bird.

Ee

easy   It is **easy** to make friends.

213

Ff

farm   Much of our food grows on a **farm**.

forest   A **forest** has many trees.

funny   You are **funny** when you hop like a frog.

Gg

goose   The **goose** took a swim on the lake.

Hh

hungry   I eat when I am **hungry**.

I i

idea   It is a smart **idea** to eat good foods.

J j

juggle   If you **juggle** the eggs, you may break them.

K k

ketchup   He likes **ketchup** on his potatoes.

kinds   There are many different **kinds** of food.

Ll

laugh　　I **laugh** when I hear something funny.

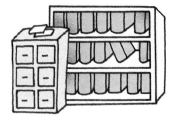

library　　The **library** is full of good books.

light　　It is **light** when the sun is out and dark when it is not.

Mm

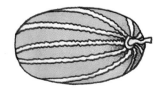

melon　　A **melon** is good to eat.

millions　　There are **millions** of stars in the sky.

Nn

nest   A bird makes a **nest** to live in.

nose   My **nose** is on my face.

notice   I **notice** that I have a hole in my shoe.

Oo

open   I will **open** the window because I am hot.

over   I saw a bird fly **over** my house.

Pp

pants   When it is cold I put on long **pants**.

pretend   When I play, I **pretend** to be a monster.

promise   When I make a **promise**, I have to keep it.

Qq

quick   If you are **quick**, you can run fast.

quit   Don't **quit** until you try your best.

Rr

rain   I get wet when I walk in
                the **rain**.

river   A **river** is water that goes
                to the sea.

room   There is **room** for one more.

Ss

search   When you lose something,
                you can **search** for it.

sled   We can ride a **sled** when
                it snows.

swallow   A **swallow** is a kind of bird.

219

Tt

thought   I **thought** of a way to help Pat.

three   **Three** is one more than two.

turnip   The **turnip** grows under the ground.

Uu

understand Now that I can read, I can **understand** this book.

upon   She sat **upon** the rock.

Ww

weather   In cold **weather** it can
              snow.

whisper   She cannot hear me when
              I **whisper**.

window   I open the **window** to let
              the air in.

Yy

year   Last **year** I was six, and
              now I am seven.

Word List

Word List